# CALENDARS

*Andreea Iulia Scridon*

ISBN: 978-1-915079-34-3

Cover designed by Aaron Kent

Edited and typeset by Aaron Kent

Broken Sleep Books Ltd
Rhydwen,
Talgarreg,
SA44 4HB
Wales

# Contents

# Calendars

Andreea Iulia Scridon

To Gabi

## Gatsby gazing over West Egg

That little green light
across Facebook Messenger,

online....

## Diogenes

I'm not looking for a husband
nor to reduce my brain cells

I'm rather the follower of Diogenes
looking for a friend
by candlelight

## *The three graces*

love
motherhood
loss

# Short poem

I don't understand
that shadow of sadness
in her eyes

## Imagine being a tree

people cutting their names into your flesh
inside a heart

## Confusion

I thought I heard your footsteps
approaching closer and closer
but it was only my heart
beating against the pillow

## The stars in Florida

are like cystic acne
so many of them
and just as human
blinking in
and out

# UNICORNUCOPIA

I.

They made Notre Dame from a thousand oaks a thousand years ago.
Flame!
Such a pretty word
for something so destructive.

## II.

Tightening the shoelaces of your mercy
as you rush past beggars, young and old,
rushing to feed the abominable cynicism
that lives in your basement,

far you have travelled
to taste the charm
of summer's empire and dominion,
these days of fading august,

far you have travelled
to hold Planet Venus
like a football between your knees,

far you have travelled
to see the hours of the year drip past,
long have you adhered to the bizarre honour
of failing to forget,

and your heart
is now hardened like a horseshoe.

# III.


See how the dust of old Paris heaves up
like an absinthe hangover, over the new.
you had a normal childhood,
your parents tell you,
even though you know
that wasn't the case at all.
how sinister, how funerary –
like the fireworks that scared
the bats out of the trees,
and how those bats blighted your sight
and how those bats eclipsed the fireworks
and smattered them into a million pieces.
Gloom, like disease, made itself at home
in the armchair of the body.

In the after-silence, the city strikes you
as emptier than the cemetery at night,
as it wasn't only you that had left it permanently,
as if its entire population had followed suit.

In the butterfly house,
you rediscover the woolly-mammoth brown of those eyes
under the microscope, examining the polyphemus moth
and just beyond the netted veil, the factory-made gossamer
for safekeeping, the Morpho butterfly loses control of her
movements like a frightened lamb, paralyzed by the memento
mori of the insectarium so close by, but still flying, still flying,
while your heart is shredded by the infantile joy of the Orthodox
priest, smiling, following the beating of their wings towards the sky

and for all this leaden absence, you keep your wonder like a locket,
you are young and still believe in people, botanical and fecund:

you have never seen an iron chain break!

## IV.

As Notre Dame was burning,
what a tree full of apples you were,
what elderflower blossom you were,
what astronaut juice you were,

as Notre Dame was burning,
what suave nightmare you were,
what passing of years you were,

what a Penelope you were
as you tangled and untangled
the white earbuds
from your lover's jacket pocket,
as Notre Dame was burning,
what absolute
what utter wreckage
blazing.

# V.

When did you become such a Marquis de Sade,
when did you become such poisonous prunes?

When did you become such a State Duma,
when did you become such non-ischemic cardiomyopathy?

There's a single pore on every pore,
a single planet in every universe,
the spiky yet silky hair of the brunette –

the disturbingly visible blue veins
on the neck, breasts, and thighs, the body
a boat with a glass bottom
through which you can see all marine life.

The solar system of the blisters on the feet.
If you'd expose those veins to air, they'd be coral...
*but I don't want to think about that now.*
This poor body, which this body has mercy for.

The softness of the skin behind the knees,
the fruit-like roughness of the front of the calf,
exposed to the sun and the wind,
the skin taut over the bone,

the blunt of every step forward.
How long can it step forward?
Only girls are eternally cold.
Their hearts have a fruitlike roughness,

still fuzzed,
still furry.
Now do you see
how everything is interconnected –

how the stones of these memories
will smooth into facelessness
as time ebbs back and forth
like a creaking swing over them

how they'll grow moss
when I'm in the ground?

I will be the border rock

between this world and the forest beyond:
it's not love if it's not a crucial period in history,
it's not love
if it isn't the only thing beyond
the creaking of the coffin's lid shut.

# VI.

My planet is the bluest hydrangea.
If you drill me to the bottom of my planet,
you'll find a brain inside.
That brain thinks about me all the time,
just as my brain upstairs
thinks about my planet all the time.
But that brain inside my planet
isn't like a human brain or animal brain,
a hardened piece of gum travelled by rivulets,
a conquistador's map.

It's an obscure gestation, that brain of mine,
it's a liturgical tapestry, an essential tremor of beauty,
great stars of gold fall on the olive earth,
it has a zoomorphic door handle
and seven spy holes, it's erotic pathos
and well-behaved baroque, there are
hummingbirds in straitjackets,
the Oronoco flows from every tap,
it's an absolute work of art,
at the watershed between
tradition and innovation,
made by strong and convincing
people, people who are capable of change
in the good sense of the term, it's –

it's sad that we're apart
but if we weren't apart,
we wouldn't have anything to long for,
nothing to pine away and lose weight for,
and our love would die, decompose,
its entire body would turn the colours of a bruise,
like a monastic painting:
violet-blue, pear-yellow,

one by one and limb by limb,
and gradually dissipate, becoming one with the earth,
like Russians
when they drink.
Like Russians who say
that true love
is the name of the baby
never taken to term...

# CALENDARS

*Mințile mi s-au smintit*
*Unghile mi s-au tocit,*
*Tălpile mi s-au belit,*

*Potecile'n crucișând,*
*Buturugile izbind*
*Și glodurile lovind.*

*Nu știu alții cum găsesc*
*Și pe placul lor iubesc,*
*Ca mine nu jinduiesc.*


*My mind has gone astray*
*My nails have ground away*
*My soles have given way,*

*Crossing walks,*
*Smacking rocks,*
*And hitting blocks.*

*I don't know how others reap*
*The love that I cannot keep,*
*Only I am made to weep.*

— Anton Pann, "Song of Longing" ("Cântec de Dor")
from *The Hospital of Love* (*Spitalul Amorului*), 1852

# *A part of me*

does worry that neither of us will ever be able to leave this place.
It's some time now that I've been living in your head, quite on your benevolence
or perhaps the indolent procrastination of a somewhat kinder landlord
than others.
Strangely, you don't seem to mind that I make of you my medicine cabinet,
that I tear down the walls around here and put up kitschy wallpaper.
In order to get with the times, I've had a sex change from nymphet to CCTV
and, in my spare time, am your eyes.
To escape the impossibility of our perfection,
a dog that I baptized "loneliness in two"
(or maybe just the sadness of the past, which, I was surprised to find,
carries on even when you are "very much in love"),
I spend my days painting frescos on the wall:
"angels playing music", already faded. When it grows dark,
I take the nail supplements poorly and put on my Disney princess
dress, the itchy one, sit down with my hands in my lap,
and wait for the room to tremble as you begin to speak.

## *Nimbus*

I took off my nimbus,
laid it down on the carpet
and smiled in slant:
here you are,
this is my home,
I said,
as to the weary traveller

but perhaps instead
I should have broken the orb in two
so that the grace that surrounds us
would begin to grow contours
like a blanket
over a hunchbacked child

## Cantata

Uterus, drugged oracle, sends twice
her interstellar messages
from the other side of paradise:

as sure as Christian reprobation, I am predestined for your
children, ill-chanced to mother this love's amputee,
detached from any berth of tenable reality

unannounced to the unknowing, mantled presence consigning,
you've stood lighthouse, Polar Star,
I'm Balthazar, Melchior and Gaspar.
Will I still tightrope the berms of your dreams,
when a horsehair noose hangs us both from their beams?
relaxed as a valerian-smoking octopus, your mind my home,
when we are married to others in our gloam?

You'll be bald, an old baby, your wife faded, still in love with you
I'll be tight-lipped, wedded too, to all I promised I would never do:

my errors lined up Matryoshka on the windowsill,
I weigh them in my palm like a beaded string of pearls
they glow around my neck
in talismanic order
with the vague lustre of regret.

All the words I never said,
        all the things I never did,

you, angel from bottom to top, my nightmare
and daymare, with your worn-out face and worn-out hair,
from inside out, from upside down –
name me as you like

but do not name me yours,
I am the poet of lost love, wool socks, and dull hues,
What's left of my face
is now the mutest trace,
I cannot be anyone's muse.

## *Pavane*

Farewell Bloomsbury,
farewell to your cherry trees,
cadavers riding down the underground sea
down to Kensington's astronomy,
its summer twilights ambergris,
flowering dishonestly
with time's passage as sole solvency:

follow the infernal tedium of family vacation l
ong siestas in the long summer of recuperation,
follow heat, the sun considers suicide,
it rains solar, drops of gold dribble side by side,
July's a month too flaxen and alive
to await responses that won't arrive

a little boy in my neighbourhood has your name
it flits from the wings of one's child's voice
to my windowpane. I watch them, here by choice

as I spend the rest of summer in churlish tones of apricot,
lengthy as chewing gum pulled taut
from the pavement by the sole on an unlucky spot
my fingers clinging to the curtain as to a slingshot –

perhaps I disappointed
beyond all measure and still
lovers, like Christ, are gracious
they try again,
try again

## Futile feathers

No, nothing lasts at all:
things that fly must fall,

though not all those who have fallen have flown
as I should carve on my wishbone,

morse-code it, brand or epitaph this broken fissure
a Mary Bloody Mary, a Xerox copy luckless figure

with a bad reputation,
hollowed bones and a breathless palpation,

as heavy hearts are not
for the birds who fly over the afterthought

of the lilac over the brick wall, my closing hope
that the cat tightropes
as I take the same coffee every day and, I admit, mope

anywhere at the end of all subway lines
a pervert voyeur on knees with cruel signs
before the keyhole of happier hours

and naturally night
seeking compassionate figures for foresight,
at least a weak light

though perhaps it is best
that the lonesome opportunistic forager should rest

molt out of my lovely plumage
or rather my palms
should fly to my eyes
for the robin's still profile against the pavement
      how good its eyes are,
      like those of toy soldiers
           and an orphan feeling for me today,
                like Christmas decorations in August

# *Gloss*

We had our way of speaking in gloss,

*One day things will become clear to you*, means
*I am a coward*,
but so am I,
so am I.

*I will remember you*, means
*I am very afraid.*

Some words are universal:
you are very clever,
but so am I,
so am I,
and I know
that you can impart them where they fit.

For this reason, *I love you*
means, in fact, that you do not.
But so do I,
so do I.

## Sonnet

Again we missed each other on this track,
outran each other, or simply lacked synchronization
sadness, after all, won't turn the calendar on its back,
regrets are useless once you've passed your destination.

I am said to be unpunctual, ill at ease,
and, more often than I'd admit, unreasonably upset,
at times Carmelite, a little bit Siamese,
no good at catching butterflies in my net.

but here's my message of hope: if you come to divine
the scent reserved for nocturnal visitors by white flowers
you'll find that love, like wine,
is at its best in more mature hours.

This is why I wait
and shake the sea gate.

## The maroon

I will ask you to refrain
from entering my thoughts in early morning
anchor or woman half goddess and half nothing
that you grip and release
the animal devoured
moors and unmoors herself

I've been in love enough
to recognise the symptoms:
it is grave, you haven't much time left,
but for your survival,
remember remember remember two things:
jealousy does well in its personal amniotic
fluid, those who curse others
are predestined for perdition

this is where I catch you,
arrest your flight, rare bird
shifting transparent, here and there,
iridescent, in mirrors I have made

I will reach out a hand to you –
do not tie yourself to me.
Have courage,
fold yourself small,
be strong, too small

for long times –
calendars as long and mournful as their sorrowful vowels,
love is the needle that pierces the skin
in minor chord.

It is uncertainty
that falls, petal after petal,
to my most shaded end
mounts soft in the darkness,
various dusks.
I do not know why I pave entire roads in the distance between us.
Forgive me.

## *On pain*

What weight your presence gives the days
for that I braille-tap on my heart,
the poor cripple inside:
stay away from the lucky,
the life-laureled and lullabied,
unbearable here
unbearable gone,
they are not for the vulnerable,
not for the likes of you.

What weigh your presence gives the days:
small stones tucked into my pockets,
perfect to cup in my palms,
perfect to weigh me down.

# *Madrigal*

Can you hold wake with a broken clock? That natural nocturne
of Thursday evening, and yet I'm poised
behind the tasselled red brocade of insanity w
ithout a way to count the hours,
he will metamorphose into fata morgana, he will leave me

seeking another kind of clock,
gazing out the window, the misty window of the moon,
serene, post-mortem, subjugative.
Vanitas mundi: the magic cinnamon air of the vape
that I allow to be puffed into my face

just another humiliation
I'd cut him in half like a Kinder egg,
eat his right side and build a toy out of his left,
a carnivorous vamp like her

in his absence, I go through his things
for the ghost of the woman he still loves.
Now I know her face better than he has,
I have studied it, seeking to estrange myself,
seeking to seek myself,
I can trace its pixelated perfection.

how does he remember all the colours of his childhood?
Was it Gaugin's eyes that he inherited
and failed to grow out of? he should claim his rights,
he should have signed a prenuptial agreement with birth.

When he is gone
she
keeps
me
company

# *Personal apocalypse*

I feign tiredness, I rub my eyes,
to hide the pity in those weary globes.
It is possible that Cain was unable to find his words,
that, just like his father, he stuttered before the block of his Father's brow.
I call it a glimmer of goodwill, that hesitation among the rubble.


How many times should I betray you
before your pride gives up the ghost?
There is supreme comfort
in the fatso lace doily topped armchair of self-betrayal.
You're a bracelet bought in Venice on holiday and lost at school,
a choochoo train,
a Tamagotchi that I locked in a desk drawer.
You are who you no longer are.


If God were in the room with us,
I'd ask him to cover my eyes with his hand,
like fever, like bedtime, like burial mound,
although when it comes down to it,
anxiety is like interventional radiology.


Look at me.
I'm prematurely old, like a rotten piece of cake,
and that paunchy American harvest moon that we are both under,
dead or alive,
is the luminous and happy yellow
of first date French fries.

## *Loosening and tightening*

the body a beautiful tumour,
won at chance
at a card game in lucky humour,

the ultra-violet rays in a complicit glance
allow our gazes to meet
over many miles and years by a prolonged dance

so that after our link has begun to unpleat
we violate each other with telepathy
even after our memory has melted by time's heat,

long after the clock man's melody
tips off the margins of the world, belated
once you've reached that sort of polarity,

shrunken or enlarged, emancipated,
eroded chastity belt, love is an abortion
that lasts nine months once terminated,

a birth timed from its start in reversion
before the parting signalled by the dove,
we forcepped what we could in overexertion:

your words not words of love
but meticulously architected, so that
to be indelible from my retina, ears, memory, all of

a card-castle in my larimar eye.
you were always such a cat,
evil but shy,

the expression in your eyes so labradorite,
and because it's been so long
since I last saw you, you're now drenched in pyrite,

starting to grow a halo in my soft touch
from being left in a pocket
and washed so much

does it hurt to grow a halo?
Does it pain you?

# Acknowledgments

Thank you to *Ethel Zine* for previously publishing "A part of me" and "Unicornucopia", thank you to *E Ratio Postmodern Poetry* for publishing "Gatsby gazing over West Egg", "The stars in Florida", and "Imagine being a tree". Thank you to *Sepia* for publishing "Loosening and tightening".

My gratitude also goes to Aaron Kent for his dedication to contemporary poetry.

# LAY OUT YOUR UNREST

Lightning Source UK Ltd.
Milton Keynes UK
UKHW041026080822
407000UK00003B/121